Kyrie Irving

*A biography of NBA basketball star
Kyrie Irving*

Shaun Carroll

Table of Contents

Introduction 1

Chapter 1: Who is Kyrie Irving? 3

Chapter 2: High School, College, NBA, and National Career to Date 11

Chapter 3: Famous Incidents with Kyrie Irving 31

Chapter 4: Crazy Things Kyrie Irving has Said 41

Chapter 5: Kyrie's Life Outside of Basketball 50

Chapter 6: What's Next for Kyrie Irving? 56

Conclusion 60

Introduction

Over the past decade, Kyrie Irving has become one of the most well-known names in the NBA and is now widely regarded as one of the best point guards in the league. However, he is not only well known for his basketball prowess, but also his outspoken attitude and sometimes controversial interviews.

In this book, we will cover everything there is to know about Kyrie Irving as a basketball player, and also as a man, looking deep into his NBA, College, and High School basketball careers, as well as some of his more outlandish views.

We will start by summarizing some of the critical points covered in this book, including his upbringing, his career to date, some of the defining moments of his career, some of his more interesting views and opinions, and his Australian heritage.

Then, we will look in more depth at some of these critical points, starting by focusing on his basketball career, breaking it down year by year, all the way back from his High School days to his brief time playing for the Brooklyn Nets in the 2019 season.

We will then highlight some of the incidents and controversial things that Kyrie Irving has said and done over the years that have led to him being a divisive figure for the NBA's fans.

We will then finish by talking more about Kyrie Irving, the man away from the court, before touching on what may come next for Irving, in all aspects of his life.

So, let's dive right in and learn about one of the most talented, talked about, and fascinating players in the NBA today.

Chapter 1: Who is Kyrie Irving?

Kyrie Irving is one of the most well-known NBA players for some of the incredible things he does on the court and some of the controversial things that he does off of it.

But there is so much more to Irving than just his basketball prowess. In this chapter, I will talk you through some of Kyrie's main aspects that make him who he is, before touching on each of these points and more in more detail in the following chapters.

Who Is Kyrie Irving?

Born in 1992, Kyrie Irving originates from Melbourne, Australia, and quickly rose to prominence for being a high school basketball superstar. He later played one injury-affected, yet successful, season at Duke University, before being the Cleveland Cavaliers number one pick in the NBA draft back in 2011.

In the 2016-2017 season, he partnered up with LeBron James at the Cleveland Cavaliers, and the pair took the franchise to its first-ever NBA Championship. As well as being known as a prolific scorer on the court, Irving is also famous for his starring role in the "Uncle Drew" commercials and subsequent movie, as well as making some rather controversial comments about his teammates and his beliefs on the earth being flat.

After playing for the Cleveland Cavaliers for six successful seasons, he moved the Boston Celtics under a slightly dark cloud, before making an even more controversial move to the Brooklyn Nets in 2019, after two injury-laden and underwhelming seasons with the Celtics.

High School Star & Duke University

After playing at a high level himself, Irving's father, Drederick Irving, ultimately settled in West Orange, New Jersey. From a young age, he often brought Kyrie with him to the pickup basketball matches he played in.

Having played the sport and been around basketball from a very young age, Kyrie quickly became a star at the local high school, Montclair Kimberley Academy. Not a well-known basketball school, he then moved to St. Patrick, where he won a state championship and many other individual accolades.

He went on to play for Duke University, becoming one of the few freshman point guards to play under Mike Krzyzewski, a famous college basketball coach. He started brightly, but a foot injury ultimately kept him out for three months of the season. Despite only playing 11 times that season, he showed enough potential for Cleveland to pick him as their number one draft pick in 2011.

Stardom & Championship in Cleveland

The Cavaliers were coming off a poor season the year before. However, Irving proved to be a shining light for the franchise early on, winning Rookie of the Year. He was also named the MVP in the Rising Stars Challenge.

He was starting to make a name for himself due to his outstanding dribbling skills and his ability to make acrobatic shots. Irving was quickly becoming talked about as one of the best guards in the league, was selected for the All-Star team in 2013, and was named MVP in the All-Star game the year after.

In the summer of 2013, LeBron announced that he would be moving back to Cleveland along with the impressive forward, Kevin Love. The Cavaliers won the NBA finals in 2016 against the Golden State Warriors, after missing out against the same team the year prior in 2015.

Boston Celtics

After an extremely successful six seasons at the Cavaliers, which included four All-Star appearances, three NBA finals, and an NBA championship, Irving requested a trade and moved the Boston Celtics in 2017.

Irving started exceptionally well at his new franchise, despite the odd injury here and there, before having his season cut short in March 2018 due to a knee injury that required surgery.

Irving was fit again by the time the new season rolled around. However, the team struggled to live up to the hype surrounding them. Over the season, Irving got himself into a lot of trouble with the media regarding his comments about re-signing and his public dressing down of his teammate's performances.

Brooklyn Nets

In the summer of 2019, both Kevin Durant and Kyrie Irving announced they had signed for the Brooklyn Nets. It was expected that these two powerhouses teaming up would transform the Nets into an exceptionally high performing team.

Irving backed up all of the pre-game talk when he scored 50 points on debut, however again, his season was hampered by injuries. Initially, he missed several games with a shoulder injury before returning and scoring 54 points. He then sustained another injury the next day, and he had to have surgery on his surgery, ruling him out for the season.

Shoes and 'Uncle Drew'

In December 2014, after already becoming an All-Star in just his fourth NBA season, Irving hit another milestone, this time off the court. He received his own signature shoe by Nike, called the "Kyrie 1."

Since then, Irving has taken up a couple of opportunities to express his designs and feelings through his footwear line. These signature lines included film quotes from Whiplash as well as a line of shoes using TV themes *Friends* and *Spongebob Squarepants*, the latter of the two selling out in under an hour.

On top of partnering with Nike, Irving also started endorsing Pepsi Max back in 2012. That year, we saw the first installment of the "Uncle Drew" commercials, where he is seen as a grumpy old man who bangs on about everything being better back in his day, while he beats younger players in a basketball match.

This concept was so successful that it saw a series of other TV adverts follow off the back of it, before it was announced in 2017 that "Uncle Drew" was going to come out as a feature-length film. In the film, Irving starred alongside Chris Webber, Shaquille O'Neal, and Reggie Miller, and it came to cinemas in 2018, achieving modest reviews and revenue.

Trade from Cleveland to Boston

Irving's trade from Cleveland to Boston is one of his most controversial moves and will be covered in more detail later in this book. After appearing in three NBA finals in a row, it came as a shock when Irving requested his trade the following summer.

He was then traded to the Celtics for Jae Crowder, Ante Zizic, and Isaiah Thomas, although the Celtics also had to provide two draft picks as Isaiah failed a medical.

While many were confused as to why he would choose to move from such a successful franchise, it became clear that he had grown frustrated with playing second fiddle to LeBron James, and wanted to move teams so that he could lead his own franchise and be the main man again, like he was before LeBron had returned to Cleveland.

Irving's Flat Earth Theory

One of the most controversial things to happen to Kyrie Irving off the court occurred in February 2017, when Irving turned heads by expressing his views that he believed the earth is not round, and that it is actually flat.

On the "Road Trippin" podcast, he insisted that there was plenty of evidence that this was true, but that people of power and wealth were preventing that information coming to light.

These comments made by Irving quickly went viral, which led to many fans wondering what was going on in Irving's brain. Irving later backtracked on these comments, stating that it was an "exploitation tactic" to prove how the media can attempt to demonize anyone that challenges the status quo, and went on to say people shouldn't just accept what they have been taught or been told. All very confusing stuff!

Mom & Dad

As we have already touched on, Irving is not the first basketball player in his family. His father, Drederick Irving, was also a well-respected basketball player in his own right before Kyrie was born. He was an All-City selection when he was a student at Adlai Stevenson High School, located in the Bronx, and he also found success playing at Boston University, setting the record as the University's all-time leading scorer, back in 1988.

He never quite reached the heights of the NBA, though, and instead played for the Bulleen Boomers for several years, out in Australia. While playing basketball at Boston University, he met Elizabeth Larson, who was part of the university volleyball team and a pianist. He married her, and they moved back to the USA (to Seattle) before they both moved to Australia for Drederick to pursue his basketball career. It was during their time in Australia that Kyrie was born. Elizabeth, unfortunately, passed away at just 29 years old, due to contracting sepsis.

Australian Roots & International Competition

Kyrie was born in Melbourne, Australia, as his dad continued his local hoops career. However, he didn't stay there for long, as his dad took his sister and Kyrie back to the USA when he was just two years old. He did keep his dual passport, though, allowing him to play for either Australia or America when he grew up.

When the time arose for Irving to choose a national team, he did consider playing for Australia, but ultimately chose Team USA, claiming a gold medal at the Olympics and at the FIBA world cup.

Personal

When it comes to his personal life, Irving recently turned vegan before the beginning of the 2017-2018 season and became a father himself back in November 2015.

He has also made contributions to The Shared Grief Project, which helps highlight the stories of professional athletes who have suffered from the loss of loved ones but have still gone on to make something out of their lives.

Chapter 2: High School, College, NBA, and National Career to Date

High School Career

Kyrie Irving's illustrious basketball career began at Montclair Kimberley Academy, playing for the high school team in his freshman and sophomore years. He managed to score 26.5 points per game over those years, 10.3 assists per game, 4.8 rebounds per game, and even 3.6 steals. So impressive were his statistics that he quickly became just the second person in the school's history to score 1,000 points for the high school team.

As for team accolades, he helped Montclair Kimberley Academy to their first-ever New Jersey Prep B state title in his sophomore year. To continue progressing his basketball career, he decided the best option for him was to transfer high schools to play at a higher level, and so he moved to St. Patrick High School. Due to the transfer, he missed out on the first month of the season, before finally teaming up with Michael Kidd-Gilchrist, who was being touted as one of the best players of the 2011 class.

In his first year at St. Patrick High School, Irving averaged 17 points, six assists, five rebounds, and two steals per game, helping the team progress to their third New Jersey Tournament of Champions, which they won for the third time in four years.

By August 2009, he had been selected to play for the USA East, where he and his teammates went on to win the Nike Global Challenge. He was named the tournament MVP, averaging over 21 points and four assists per game.

However, the following season, St. Patrick High School was banned from competing for the state championship after being found to have started practice earlier than the rules permit you to do so in high school basketball. Despite this, St. Patrick set a 24-3 record and went on to win the Union County Championship. Irving finished that season with an average of 24 points, seven assists, and five rebounds per game.

In January 2010, Kyrie Irving was picked for the Junior National Team. They competed in Oregon in the Rose Garden, at the Nike Hoop Summit in April. He also got to play in the Jordan Brand Classic and the 2010 All-American game.

He also went to the Under-18 FIBA Americas Championship with the national team in June 2010, where he won a gold medal.

College Career

After finishing his high school career, Irving announced on ESPNU that he would be committing to play for Duke the following season. Under head coach Mike Krzyzewski, Kyrie Irving averaged 17.4 points across the first eight games of the season, shooting at 53.2%, providing over five assists a game, 1.5 steals, and 3.8 rebounds.

He was playing well and was a leading candidate to become the NCAA Freshman of the Year, before he suffered a severe ligament injury to his toe while playing the ninth game of the year. He managed to get back to being fit for the first round of games in the NCAA Tournament. Duke was able to advance to the Sweet Sixteen knockout stages, falling to Arizona. Irving scored 28 points in that game, which ended up being his final game for Duke.

Cleveland Cavaliers 2011–2017

2011–12 Season: Rookie of the Year

Before the 2011-2012 season, Kyrie Irving declared that he was going to pass up the last three seasons he had of eligibility for college basketball, instead choosing to enter himself into the

2011 NBA draft, in the hope of being selected by one of the NBA teams for the coming season, ideally early on in the draft.

As it happened, he was then picked by the Cleveland Cavaliers, as their first choice pick overall. The previous season, Cleveland had recorded just 19 wins and 62 losses in the season, which was the worst season they had endured since 2002-2003.

Cleveland was keen to get results out of Irving early and try and get back to their winning ways of the past. Their pick paid off as well, as Kyrie Irving went on to be selected for the Rising Stars Challenge in 2012, playing for Team Chuck. He went on to register 34 points in that game, with a 100% record from outside the arc, scoring eight three-pointers from eight attempts, gaining MVP honors in the process.

In the 2012 season, he also claimed NBA Rookie of the Year, with a resounding 117 of the 120 votes going in his favor. In the NBA All-Rookie First Team, this made him the only player who had been unanimously selected.

Overall, in the 2012 season, Kyrie Irving had an 18.5 point average, averaged 5.4 assists per game, and had a 46.9 shooting percentage, with it being 39.9 percent from three.

2012–13 Season: First All-Star Season

After an outstanding Rookie season, the entire NBA fan base were eager to see what Kyrie Irving could achieve in his second season at the Cleveland Cavaliers. Unfortunately, they had to wait a little longer than planned to find out. On July 14th, 2012, in a training session in Las Vegas, Irving suffered a hand injury. He ultimately needed surgery to resolve the issue and get himself fit for the season ahead.

At the time, Irving said he needed to become more responsible for his health, and that he was disappointed that the incident occurred, but that he would learn from the situation going forwards.

But that wasn't to be the end of Kyrie Irving's injuries in the 2012-2013 season. Once the season began, Irving landed awkwardly in a losing effort against the Dallas Mavericks, injuring his index finger as a result. This didn't prevent him from starting in the next game for Cleveland, but he struggled to play through the pain and ultimately missed out on the following three weeks of basketball.

When he returned to action, he was desperate not to spend any more time on the sidelines and was itching to play a crucial role in the Cavaliers push to make the playoffs. After suffering a face injury where he fractured a bone, he decided to play with a face mask on, and the decision paid off on the court. Irving went on to notch up 41 points in a game against the Knicks, which at the time was a career high. It also made him the youngest person in the NBA's history to score more than 40 points at Madison Square Garden, beating Michael Jordan's record by a year, which was set in 1985.

The rest of the season continued without any further injuries, and Irving played well enough to be chosen to play in that year's All-Star Game, which was also the first time Kyrie had been selected as an All-Star. He managed a total of 15 points on the night, as well as three rebounds and four assists.

On top of the NBA All-Star game, he also took part in the Rising Stars Challenge for a second consecutive year, this time playing for Team Shaq. Although he was able to score an impressive 32 points, his team ended up losing that game. The final All-Star Weekend competition Irving took part in during 2012 was the Three-Point Contest, where he hit 23 points in the last round of the competition, winning the competition.

Irving's season ended with an average of 22.5 points, 3.7 rebounds, 5.9 assists, and 1.5 steals per game.

2013–14 Season: All-Star Game MVP

In the 2013-2014 season, Irving was chosen by fans to be a starting point guard in the NBA All-Star game, representing the Eastern Conference. In that game, he claimed MVP honors by scoring 31 points, and recording an impressive 14 assists, as the Eastern conference overcame the Western Conference with a 163-155 final score.

Irving set another personal milestone in late February of 2014, by scoring his first-ever triple-double. He did this by contributing ten rebounds, 12 assists, and scoring 21 points in a winning effort against the Utah Jazz. Not only was this the first triple-double of Kyrie Irving's career, but it was the first triple-double anyone had scored for the Cavaliers since March 2010! He was also able to set a new career-high points tally in an overtime loss against Charlotte, scoring an impressive 44 points in the 96-94 loss.

In the 2013-2014 season, Irving managed an average of 20.8 points, with 3.6 rebounds, 6.1 assists, and 1.5 steals per game.

2014–15 Season: First NBA Finals and Big Three Formation

The 2014-2015 season shaped up to be extremely successful for Kyrie Irving and the Cleveland Cavaliers.

Prior to the start of the season, Kyrie Irving signed a new contract with the Cavaliers. The five-year contract extension was worth an eye-watering $90-million, and shortly followed the news that Lebron James would return to the Cavaliers for the upcoming season. Not only that, but Cleveland had also been able to land

Kevin Love from Minnesota. The three players became known in Cleveland as the "Big Three," and expectations were high.

Despite these expectations and high-profile starters, they suffered a poor start to the season, opening with a 5-7 record. However, after that, they went eight-games without losing, where Kyrie Irving was able to average 19.3 points and record a 37-point game in the process in December when they played the New York Knicks. All signs were pointing towards a smooth trip to the playoffs.

But the charge of the Cavaliers stalled again, as their winning streak ended against Oklahoma City on December 11th, and they only notched up five more wins in the month, finishing 2014 with a mediocre 18-14 win-loss record. However, one of the reasons for this was that each of the leading three players missed some games in December, which left the Cavaliers lacking potency and creativity on the court. With all three fit again in the new year, there was still hope that their season would be a success.

Optimism grew as the Cavaliers started with a win on January 2nd, with Irving putting up 23 points, and Love scoring 27 points. However, in the next game, Irving could only manage six points before being pulled from the floor in the third quarter as he was suffering from tightness in his lower back. The Cavaliers lost that game, and Irving also had to sit out the following game, which was against Philadelphia, making his return to action in the game after, where they battled the Houston Rockets. In the comeback game, Irving scored 23 points in the first half, which at the time was a career high for a single half of basketball. He finished the game with 38 points, but the Cavaliers' woes continued, as they lost the game and had now recorded seven losses in their last nine games.

The Cavaliers had moved to 19-20, and things were starting to look ominous. Just when they needed them to, though, Irving and James stepped up and took Cleveland on a winning streak which lasted twelve games and put them back into the mix at the top of the conference. In this twelve game streak, Irving's average shot to 24.5 points per game, scoring 55 points in one game against Portland, which was a new career high. He hit 11 three-pointers, which was a record for the Cleveland Cavaliers, on top of his 55 points being the second highest in their history, and the highest number of points scored in a home game. Twenty-eight of those points came in the first half, which was yet another career high.

But Irving went one better in March 2015 when he scored 57 points; this tally also included a three-point shot after the buzzer, which took the Cavaliers to overtime, in a game they ultimately were able to win versus the Spurs. This broke a record that had stood for over 50 years, with it being the most points anyone had scored against a reigning champion. It also eclipsed the 56-point record LeBron held for the most points in a game for Cleveland.

In total, Irving was able to assist the Cavaliers to 24 wins from their remaining games, which led to them finishing the Eastern Conference season as the number two seed, boasting a 53-29 record. This took Irving to the playoffs for the first time in his career. In his first game, he provided 30 points in a 113-100 winning effort against the Celtics. He managed to play a vital role in the other playoff games as well, ultimately helping Cleveland reach the NBA Finals. This was only the second time they had been able to reach the NBA Finals in franchise history.

Unfortunately for Irving, he suffered a fractured kneecap during the NBA Finals in the first game versus the Golden State Warriors. This meant he missed the remaining games in the series and was out of action for three to four months as a result.

The Cavaliers went on to lose the series in six games, and Irving was left to rue what might have been.

2015–16 Season: NBA Championship

On the back of a successful 2014-2015 season, Irving and his teammates were determined to perform even better the next season. However, due to the severe knee injury he had sustained in the NBA finals, Kyrie wasn't able to take to the court for the start of the season, instead making his season debut in December. He played a total of 17 minutes in the game, scoring 12 points. In early January, he went on to score 32 points, a season high, in the Cavaliers victory over the Washington Wizards. He also scored 32 points in February, along with a career high 12 assists, when Cleveland beat Sacramento. Just two days later, he went one better and scored 35 points in a win over the Lakers.

After finishing as the second seed in the Eastern Conference the previous year, this year, the Cavaliers finished with an impressive 57-25 record, making them the first seed. In game one of the playoffs, Irving scored 31 points, before tying that record again in game three, against the eight-seed team, the Detroit Pistons. They brushed past their opponents in the playoffs to reach the NBA finals for a second consecutive year, where once again, they found themselves facing the Golden State Warriors.

Initially, Irving struggled with his shooting, scoring on only 7 of his 22 attempted shots, finishing with 26 points. The Cavaliers went on to lose game one, before dropping to 3-1 in the series after losing game four.

In game five, Irving and LeBron stepped up, with both of them firing home 41 points and guiding their team to a win, taking the contest to a game six. This was the first time in NBA Finals history that more than one teammate had scored 40 points.

Irving stepped up again in game six, scoring a three-point shot with less than a minute left on the game clock. The Cavaliers won game six and went on to win the decider, making them the first team to ever win the NBA finals from being 3-1 behind, beating the Golden State Warriors, and ending a 52 year wait for a major sports championship in Cleveland.

2016–17 Season: Final Season with the Cavaliers

It is a tradition in the NBA to be given your championship ring before the first game of the following season. Kyrie Irving celebrated the occasion, scoring a game high 29 points in the Cavaliers victory against the New York Knicks. Just three days later, he followed that up with another 26 points and scored a three-pointer with less than a minute to go, giving his team the lead against the Toronto Raptors.

In late November, Kyrie Irving went on a hot streak in the final quarter of their win against the Philadelphia 76ers, scoring 19 of his 39 game points in the quarter, guiding his team over the line. He continued to perform in early December, scoring 20 points or more for the tenth game running. In late December, he managed 31 points on top of a career high assist tally of thirteen, in a victory against the Milwaukee Bucks.

Keen to continue his high-performance into the following year, Irving scored a season high 49 points against the New Orleans Pelicans. Thirty-five of these came in the second half. However, the Cavaliers ultimately lost the game, taking them to five losses in their last seven games.

A couple of weeks later, Irving set himself a new career best for assists, racking up 14 in a comfortable win against the Minnesota Timberwolves. He also bagged 43 points for his team in early March, in their high-scoring victory against the Atlanta Hawks. Kyrie followed that up with another more than 40-point game in the same month, scoring 46 points against the Los Angeles Lakers in a game the Cavaliers won 125-120. He then managed 45 points in a tightly contested overtime loss versus Atlanta.

It's no surprise that these performances helped the Cleveland Cavaliers to another Eastern Conference Finals versus the Boston Celtics. In game four, Kyrie Irving put up 42 points in the Cavaliers win, which was a career-high for him in the playoffs.

He also scored 24 points in game five, which helped the Cleveland Cavaliers beat the Celtics and take the series 4-1. As a result, Cleveland claimed their third Eastern Conference title in a row, and a third season competing in the NBA Finals. However, things didn't quite go to plan, as they lost all three of the first finals games before Irving managed 40 points in the fourth game, which kept the series alive at 3-1. Despite last year's heroics, it wasn't meant to be this year, and Cleveland lost game five of the series and the Golden State Warriors took back their crown as the NBA champs.

Boston Celtics 2017–2019

2017–18 Season

To the surprise of a lot of the NBA fanbase, Kyrie Irving asked the Cleveland Cavaliers to trade him in July 2017. It was reported at the time that Irving was becoming frustrated with LeBron James being the focal point of the team, and instead wanted to play somewhere where he was the leader of the group instead. By the end of August, the Cleveland Cavaliers had granted him his wish and traded him to the Boston Celtics.

In return, they received the services of Jae Crowder, Isaiah Thomas, and Ante Zizic, and also a first-round draft pick. A week later, the Boston Celtics also allowed the Cleveland Cavaliers to have a second-round draft pick to finalize the trade, as Thomas had failed the physical test and was no longer eligible.

Interestingly, Kyrie Irving's debut for the Boston Celtics came against the Cleveland Cavaliers. On debut, he managed a total of 10 assists and 22 points, but they lost the game 102-99. At the buzzer, he had the opportunity to shoot a three and tie the game up, taking it into overtime. Unfortunately, he missed, and his debut against his former team ended in defeat.

In late October, Irving put up 24 points for the third game in a row, in a winning effort against the San Antonio Spurs. This game was particularly significant, as the Boston Celtics had not beaten the San Antonio Spurs since 2011. In total, Irving managed an impressive 128 points in his first half a dozen games as a Celtic player, which was the highest tally since Ray Allen and Garnett both put up 131 in 2007.

He also broke another Boston Celtics record, scoring 245 points in his first 11 games, more than any other player had managed in the franchise's history. This also occurred during Boston's ninth win in a row, taking the team to a 9-2 record to start the season.

In late November, Kyrie put up 47 points, a season high. He managed ten of these points in overtime, helping the Boston Celtics to recover from being well behind in the game, to defeat the Dallas Mavericks, taking their winning run to sixteen games in the process. Unfortunately, the Celtics then lost to the heat two days after, ending their impressive winning streak.

Kyrie Irving started 2018 in similarly impressive scoring form, scoring 40 points in a losing effort against the Orlando Magic in late January. By mid-January, the Celtics had an impressive 34-10 record. However, this loss to the Magic was their third loss in a row.

Irving managed a further 37 points in another losing effort in late January against the Golden State Warriors. In that game, he managed a total of five three-pointers. However, the winning ways soon came back to the Boston Celtics, and Irving was able to take the team to a four-game winning streak after the All-Star break, with a resounding 134-106 victory against the Charlotte

Hornets. In that game, he managed another 34 points, hitting four of his six three-point attempts before the start of the fourth quarter.

However, what was set to be one of, if not the most productive seasons of Kyrie Irving's career was cut short in March 2018. Initially, he was expected to miss around three to six weeks of action, as he had to undergo a procedure to take out a tension wire that was in his left knee.

Less than two weeks after that, he was then ruled out for the rest of the season and the postseason, as he needed four or five months to recover from another procedure, this time to take out the two screws that were in his patella. They had been placed there after the kneecap fracture he suffered during the NBA finals of 2015 to help repair the bone but had recently been causing him a lot of pain, and ultimately had served their purpose and needed to be removed.

2018–19 Season

Due to the major surgery that he had to undergo at the end of the previous season, Irving had been unable to play any competitive basketball since March, having to wait five months until the season opener in October. In his first game back, he managed just seven points and seven assists. Despite this, the Boston Celtics went on to win the game against the Philadelphia 76ers,

105-87. There was clearly some nerves and some rustiness, as Irving missed his first nine attempts in the game, before scoring a pair of free throws in the second half.

Through the first six games, he averaged just 14 points per game, which was significantly lower than in his first season for the Celtics. However, in a win against the Detroit Pistons on October 30th, he managed 31 points, before scoring a season high 39 points against the Phoenix Suns in a winning effort on November 8th.

He backed that up eight days later, with another season-high, scoring 43 points and bagging 11 assists in a win against the Toronto Raptors. This was also the first time that Kyrie Irving had scored more than 40 points and also provided more than ten assists in one game. No one had achieved that feat at the Boston Celtics since Antoine Walker did it, way back in 2001.

He scored a further 38 points on December 12th, in yet another overtime win, this time against the Washington Wizards. He followed that up with 40 points and ten rebounds a couple of weeks later, and 26 points in a game on December 29th, where 22 of those points came in the second half. He also managed a season-high 13 assists in that winning effort against the Memphis Grizzlies, which was just one shy of his all-time personal best.

He smashed that record out of the park on January 16th, when he managed 18 assists and 27 points in a win against the Toronto

Raptors. He set another career-best five days later when he recorded eight steals in a win against the Miami Heat. He followed these personal milestones up with his 11th double-double of points and assists in a losing effort against the Golden State Warriors, scoring 32 points and providing ten assists. He also became the first Celtic player to hit that many double-doubles for almost 25 years, after Larry Bird achieved the feat in the 1986-1987 season. It also matched the sixth game in a row Irving had scored 25 points, a personal milestone.

In the middle of March, he notched up his second-ever triple-double, scoring 41 points, ten rebounds, and 12 assists, in a closely fought game against the Sacramento Kings. He became the first Boston Celtics player since Rajon Rondo to score 30 or more points and a triple-double in one game. A couple of days later, he almost completed the feat again, scoring 30 points and 11 rebounds, but fell just short with nine assists, in a winning effort against the Atlanta Hawks.

The form of Irving and his teammates took the Celtics to the playoffs, and he became only the third player ever in Boston Celtics history to score more than twenty points, more than five rebounds, and more than five assists in a postseason debut game. They beat the Indiana Pacers in game one, and also game two of the series, as Irving notched up 37 points. They went on to advance to the second round, where Irving scored a playoff career-best of 11 assists in a win against the Milwaukee Bucks.

Unfortunately, the Celtics were not able to progress any further than round two.

Brooklyn Nets 2019–Present

Irving became a free agent before the 2019 season, and on July 7th, opted to sign for the Brooklyn Nets. He played his first game for the franchise on October 23rd, scoring an impressive 50 points, making seven assists, and eight rebounds, in a losing effort against the Minnesota Timberwolves. This made him the first man in NBA history to score 50 points in a debut match for a team. He also became just the seventh player in Brooklyn nets history to score 50 points in a single game for them.

Frustratingly though, the 2019-2020 season proved to be a stop-start one for Kyrie Irving, as he then went on to miss a total of 26 games, with an injury to his right shoulder. He scored 21 points in a winning effort on his return in January, before scoring 45 points a couple of weeks later.

The Brooklyn Nets were due to play against the New York Knicks the following day; however, after learning of Kobe Bryant's death, Irving decided not to play. On January 31st, he came back to score a season-high 54 points in a victory over the Chicago Bulls. Again, however, his season was cut short on February 20th, due to the same shoulder injury that had ruled him out for a long time earlier in the season.

National Team Career

As Irving was born in Australia, he was eligible to play for the Australian team at the 2012 Olympics, with the country keen to select him and have him pledge his services to their country. However, Irving decided he would instead focus on the USA national team, although they didn't select him for the 2012 Olympic team.

However, Irving was a part of the US national team that took part in the FIBA Basketball World Cup in 2014. He was able to assist Team USA as they went on to win a gold medal. He was so influential in that success that he was named as the MVP of the tournament.

He started each of the nine games, averaging over 12 points per game and 3.6 assists, and managed 26 points in the final of the competition. After such an impressive performance, Kyrie Irving was given the award of USA Basketball Male Athlete of the Year.

Kyrie followed that up by representing Team USA at the 2016 Olympics, where he helped them achieve a gold medal for their nation. After winning this medal, he became one of four players to win an NBA championship as well as an Olympic Gold Medal in the same year. The other three men were Michael Jordan, Scottie Pippen, and LeBron James.

Chapter 3: Famous Incidents with Kyrie Irving

While Kyrie Irving is very famous for his work on the basketball court, he is also not shy about voicing his opinions in the media and has often caused quite a few feathers to be ruffled with his antics and comments in interviews over the years. In this chapter, we will focus on some of the most intriguing and famous interviews in Kyrie Irving's career, and look at how they impacted his career and life as a result.

His Walk-Back on Boston

In 2017 Kyrie Irving was traded from the Cleveland Cavaliers to the Boston Celtics, citing his desire to step into a leadership role after his relationship with the Cleveland Cavaliers leader, LeBron James, had gone sour.

After an extremely successful start to life in Boston, Kyrie's debut season for the Celtics was cut short. Despite this, there was already a lot of hype about a contract extension the following season, due to his high-quality performances the season before. The Celtics were ready to build a squad around Kyrie Irving; all they needed from him was the commitment that he was going to be a Boston Celtics player for many years to come.

On June 14th, 2018, Kyrie Irving was coy on the subject, stating that he was focusing on the day to day work in training with the team to get back to his best for the upcoming season. Speaking to ESPN, Irving stated that he focused on health and redemption, rather than a contract extension at the Boston Celtics.

He states that he can't comment on contracts at this time, although he is sure that management from his side and Boston will discuss, he is focusing solely on bringing a championship back to the Celtics.

On September 24th, Irving spoke to Kirsten Ledlow from NBA TV, telling her he believes that Boston is the place for him. At this time, he claimed that any player would want to be a part of the Boston Celtics franchise, as they are a top-tier team in the NBA and have been set up to be a competitive team for several years.

He told NBA TV that he envisages having his shirt retired and up in the rafters when he has finished playing and that Boston Celtics is the place to elevate his game to even further greatness. At this point, all signs suggested Irving was considering resigning as a free agent on a long-term basis, although nothing was concrete.

Things went a step further on October 4th, when Irving stated categorically that he planned on signing for the following season. The only reason he hadn't done so yet was that if he waited, he would get paid more money. At this point, almost everyone believed that Irving would be a Celtics player in 2019, as rarely do players give their word in such a confident and transparent way. However, as we know, this wasn't what transpired.

Things started to change course on January 12th, after the Boston Celtics lost to the Orlando Magic, who were not a strong team that year. Irving came out and slated his teammates in an interview, claiming the younger players didn't have what it takes to win championships, and as a result he fell out with the head coach Brad Stevens. There were massive chants from the Boston fans in their next game, shouting 'Kyrie's Leaving.'

Ultimately, Kyrie Irving walked back on his promise to stay at the Celtics, instead opting to join the Brooklyn Nets. In a recent interview, Kyrie put that down to his grandfather's passing at the beginning of his last season at the Celtics. He stated that this made him re-evaluate what was important to him, and he decided he wanted to play closer to home. As he grew up in New Jersey, the Brooklyn Nets was a perfect option for him, so he chose to leave the Celtics after two, ultimately underwhelming seasons.

His Apology to LeBron

It is no secret that Kyrie Irving and LeBron James didn't always see eye to eye during their time as Cleveland Cavaliers players, with Irving often finding himself frustrated at playing what he saw as a supporting role, rather than being the leader of the team.

This frustration led Irving to switch allegiances to the Boston Celtics, but he didn't go quietly and made sure everyone knew his reasons for leaving were that he wasn't the main man at Cleveland. To LeBron's credit, he stayed professional throughout, choosing not to talk any trash in the media about his former teammate, but you could tell that there was no love lost between the pair.

This is what made it all the more surprising when Irving announced that he had reached out to LeBron in early January 2019 to apologize for his behavior while he was a Cleveland Cavaliers player.

Irving had been particularly scathing of his teammates in the news after a loss to a poor Orlando Magic side, and he stated that on reflection, this made him stop and think about what type of young player he was at Cleveland, and he didn't like what he thought.

He stated he felt the need to apologize for being a young player so eager to be the best that he wanted everything there and then. He had become obsessed with being the guy people turned to, to lead the team to a championship, and became jealous when it was clear that man was LeBron, and not him.

He went on to state that being the best player in the world and also being responsible for leading a team to glory is a niche that not every player is meant to fill, and that Lebron was a player that had the ability to do that, even when players such as himself were acting out, which is why he deems him to be one of the very best.

His Beliefs on the Shape of the Earth

In February 2017, Kyrie Irving made a statement during a podcast interview that surprised many people, stating that he outright believed the earth to be flat. There is a small percentage of people who think that the earth is not round in the shape of a globe, and that rather it is a flat shape instead.

When he was pressed later on in the interview on that statement, Kyrie Irving backtracked slightly and instead suggested that people should go out there and do some of their own research on the subject, questioning how we can be sure that the earth isn't flat.

Irving does have a tendency to be a slightly controversial figure, yet it was surprising to hear him make these statements, as the flat earth theory has been widely disproven in many scientific studies, yet no one would suggest that Irving was one of the less bright NBA players on today's roster.

In a separate interview in September that year, Irving was again asked about his views on the earth's shape, referencing the comments he had made earlier in the year. This time, however, Irving claimed that at the time, he was making a joke on the podcast and that this was mistaken as him being serious by the media, who had blown the whole thing out of proportion.

Despite so brazenly disregarding these comments in September, in June of the next year, he was pressed on the subject again by the media, where he backtracked once more and refused to say that he accepted that the world was round. He reiterated in this meeting that he thought people should go out and do their own research, claiming the education system was flawed. He quickly followed this up with an interview in October, apologizing for his comments on the earth being flat and retracting his views on this and the education system.

This wasn't the only conspiracy theory that peaked the attention of Kyrie Irving, as he has also gone on the record stating that he thinks that John F. Kennedy may have been killed by the federal reserve, and the CIA might have attempted to murder Bob Marley.

Not Wanting to be a Celebrity

When you become a professional NBA player, it doesn't necessarily turn you into a celebrity. However, there are several things that the professional players can do through their career that move them from just being a professional athlete to also being a celebrity. Some of these actions include acting in movies, promoting their name next to a brand to help it sell, and using their career in basketball to turn themselves into a brand, such as Michael Jordan with the Air Jordan brand.

Over his career to date, Kyrie Irving has completed all of these tasks, making him a celebrity as a result. That is why it came as a surprise that during his final few months as a Boston Celtics player, Kyrie Irving stated that he just wanted to focus on playing basketball and is sick of the fame and celebrity status that came with his ability on the court.

In a news conference in early 2019, Kyrie claimed that he never chose to play basketball for all of the cameras, the flashing lights, and the fame, and that he found those parts of the job quite challenging. He admitted that those were things that he strived for when he was young, but now, all he wanted to do was focus on playing basketball to the highest standard that he could.

That makes sense on paper, as many players' aims and aspirations change throughout their careers. Add to that, he was deep in the midst of potentially leaving the Celtics at this time, and there was constant media attention towards him around the subject, and you could see why he may have grown sick of the cameras.

However, fans were quick to point out that he wasn't saying he no longer wanted to be a celebrity, but rather that he never wanted to be a celebrity at any stage in his career. Fans found this hard to believe, given that even as recently as a year ago, Kyrie was out promoting a film he was starring in called Uncle Drew, and stating in interviews that he wanted to create his own TV network.

Some critics called this fickle, and many felt that if you are taking on jobs that rely on you being famous or in front of the cameras, then you are seeking celebrity status in that form to help your projects make money. If this is the case, then many fans felt Kyrie should accept that the spotlight comes with those types of career moves, and he should accept it for what it is, or stop undertaking those types of projects.

It was clear looking back that Irving's comments were more related to the constant media scrutiny he was under regarding the next stage of his career, and that he was dealing with a lot of attention on a subject that he didn't want to be drawn in on, which can understandably be very frustrating and disheartening.

His Attack on the Fans

When the Boston Celtics played the Brooklyn Nets in 2019, there seemed to be more focus on booing and jeering Kyrie Irving rather than the game itself, despite Kyrie not even being in the building on the night.

Boston won the game 121-110, but the main talking point from the game was Irving, after the Celtic fans booed him throughout the night.

Irving was not playing in the game because he had injured his shoulder earlier in the season and was missing his seventh game in a row. But that didn't stop the Boston Celtics supporters from jeering and booing him, even with him not being there. NBA fans are very passionate about their teams, and things can go awry very quickly when someone is deemed to have left on sour terms.

Not only were the home fans booing him, but they had also produced posters calling Irving a coward and had brandished them across the entrance of the arena. Some fans even went to the game wearing the No.11 jersey he wore for the Celtics, taping over the name and replacing it with "Where is?" instead. Once it was announced in the introductions that Kyrie would not be playing in the game, the initial "Kyrie Sucks" chants began to echo around the arena and appeared many times throughout the night, often when a Nets player was at the free-throw line.

Commenting on the incident, Kyrie's teammate and Nets center Jarret Allen explained he actually thought that it could have been a lot worse, and the booing probably would have been if Kyrie Irving had even been playing.

In a statement on his social media channel, Kyrie wrote that this type of stuff happens all the time, and in a long-winded message, explained that he felt there were more important things in life than basketball and that the fans needed to grow up and get a grip. As you can imagine, this didn't go down too well with many Boston Celtics fans.

Chapter 4: Crazy Things Kyrie Irving has Said

It wouldn't be fitting to have a book written about Kyrie Irving, without addressing some of the remarkable statements that he has come out with over the years. In this chapter, we have pulled together some of the craziest things that he has said over the years, apart from his comments on the earth being flat, as we have already covered those in a previous chapter.

Kyrie Irving is one of the best basketball players of his generation, but he is also one of the most controversial with some of the comments that he has made.

"I Plan on Re-Signing Here Next Year"

As we have touched on, one of Kyrie Irving's main talking points to date came in early October 2018, when he decided to announce to the world that he was going to re-sign to the Boston Celtics in 2019.

Looking back, this is not what transpired, making the statement one of the craziest things that he said. Very rarely, if ever, does a player announce almost an entire year in advance of free agency what they are going to do, as you are showing your hand and likely weakening the offers you may get.

We can only speculate about what Jeff Wechsler, Irving's agent at the time, must have thought when he saw this interview.

Kyrie Irving later went on to admit that he had been caught up in the situation's emotions and then considerably backtracked, before joining the Brooklyn Nets.

As you can imagine, this didn't go down well with the Boston Celtics fans and many neutral NBA fans, leading to him becoming a pantomime villain whenever the Nets play against the Celtics.

This hasn't seemed to have bothered Irving too much, though, as he has often stated on social media that he brushes these comments off and tells fans to focus on more important things in life than just basketball.

"I Won't Question My Teammates in Public Again"

After the Celtics were embarrassed by an inferior Orlando Magic team on January 12th, Kyrie Irving came out and made some scathing comments about his teammate's abilities, especially the younger players in the franchise, and their ability and mindset to win major championships.

He stated that he didn't feel that the younger players in the team know what is required to take a team to win the NBA finals. He mentioned to RealGM that they don't know what work it takes every day; the work required on and off the court.

The Celtics had made it to the playoffs the previous season and were only one win from appearing in the NBA finals, even without Irving as he had been injured the year prior. However, Irving thought that this success had led to expectations that the team wasn't handling well.

These comments were so important because they were made in public, where many felt they should have been kept behind closed doors and that apart from that loss, the Celtics were very much still in contention that season.

Anyone who has followed Kyrie Irving's career will know that these kinds of outlandish comments about teammates in public are not uncommon; he even made similar comments about Lebron James, one of the best of all time, while he was part of the Cleveland Cavaliers franchise.

If he was willing to call out LeBron James in public, then it should be no surprise that he lashed out with these comments about his teammate's work ethic.

"That's No. 23's Job"

A lot has been said about the issues that Kyrie Irving had at the Cleveland Cavaliers, most notably his issues with LeBron James being the focal point of the team. In interviews after this incident, Kyrie Irving has admitted that he didn't want LeBron to rejoin the Cleveland Cavaliers, as he knew that it would take a lot of the spotlight and leadership responsibilities off him.

He was proved right, as most of the Cavaliers' game revolved around LeBron James, trying to free up time and space for him to take the team to victories. After a while, and despite a lot of success with this format, this playing style started to grate on Irving, and he became more and more visibly annoyed and frustrated with the situation that he found himself in.

It wasn't that he didn't enjoy the winning run and domination that the Cavaliers were experiencing, but he was getting increasingly frustrated with all of the focus being on LeBron James both in the media and on the court, which led to some choice words in February 2017, at the Cleveland Cavaliers practice facility.

Each player has a different playing style, and Kyrie Irving is well-known to be a point guard that likes to bring the ball up the court slowly or without urgency. This isn't because he doesn't want to score quickly or play with intent; it is because he likes to take his time, soak up the atmosphere, and decide what the best play will be at this time and how he is going to execute it.

There is also something to be said for the fact that Irving liked having the ball, as, for a moment, the spotlight was on him and not LeBron. Ty Lue, the Cleveland Cavaliers coach at the time, was imploring with Irving to play quicker, asking him to bring the ball up faster, as it will allow the team to get more shots off in the game overall.

This confused Irving, as he explained to Ty Lue that, with the ball in his hand, he could get a shot off whenever he wanted, leading to Ty Lue explaining that he meant shots for his teammates, not for himself.

This is when Irving made the comment that this was LeBron's job, and not his, which further showed that Irving was annoyed that James was able to pick up the point-forward role and drop it again whenever he fancied it during games. To add insult to injury, he didn't reference LeBron by name, but instead by his jersey number.

"One of Those Generational Leaders"

This one takes a little bit of explaining, and should give you an idea about why Irving is one of the most famous NBA players for his quirky yet sometimes baffling interviews. As you well know by now, Irving isn't someone who likes to keep things to himself, and also has the required confidence that it takes to become a professional player.

After all, if you don't believe in your own abilities, then who will? However, going a step further and declaring yourself a generational leader might be a touch too far in some people's books!

But that's precisely what Kyrie Irving did in June 2018 at a red carpet event in Santa Monica, California. In an interview at the MTV Movie and TV awards, he was asked a question about his current relationship with Kehlani, the famous R&B singer and ex-girlfriend of Irving.

We should also point out here that while also saying some crazy things, Irving is very protective and kind to those around him, and does do a lot of nice things for the people in his life that he cares about. However, once the conversation gets onto the friendly gestures, you can be sure that he is also likely to follow it with a bizarre or crazy comment as well.

In this instance, the nice act was that in 2016, when he and Kehlani had broken up but not gone public with the news, she was receiving a lot of hatred online, as fans thought that she was cheating on Kyrie Irving.

Kyrie took it upon himself to address this on his own social media page, clarifying that they had, in fact, broken up, were on good terms, and that he was pleased she had moved on.

The crazy part here is that he somehow flipped the conversation into something entirely different in the interview, before calling himself a "generational leader," which was a long way from the question about his relationship with his ex-girlfriend.

"Why Would I Have To?"

In September 2017, Irving made the decision to be a guest on "First Take," the popular ESPN Morning show. The reason he wanted to go onto the show was to explain to the hosts and the fans about why he chose to request a trade that ultimately led to him moving to the Boston Celtics. He was then grilled on the show by the hosts, Max Kellerman and Stephen A. Smith, as they tried to get Irving to open up about the real reasons behind his trade from the Cavaliers to the Celtics, given all the media reports about the animosity between him and LeBron James, and how many believed that Kyrie Irving was jealous of all of the attention being on LeBron and not on his performances.

One of the questions that the hosts asked him surrounding his relationship with LeBron was whether or not he had spoken to LeBron James before making the move, or even before he handed in his request to be transferred, or whether he had done the whole thing himself and not let anyone know.

The reasons Kyrie was giving for moving did not sound like the real reasons, stated the hosts, as they pointed out that LeBron and Kyrie had gone to three NBA finals in a row as a pair, so moving to find success seemed like a strange reason to ask for a trade.

Kyrie Irving responded to the question of if he had spoken with James about the trade beforehand sharply and abruptly with, "Why would I have to?". This told the hosts and all of the viewers watching the interview everything they needed to know about the stormy relationship between the two superstars, as clearly, they were not on speaking terms.

Irving had previously passed comments on LeBron James as part of his news conference unveiling him as a Celtics player, adding that he wasn't bothered if James took the comments personally or not.

"It Connected Me More to Nikola Tesla"

In what can only be described as a bizarre interview in general, Irving made an appearance on the J.J. Redick podcast back in January 2018, and the two shared some of their more "out there" conspiracy theories.

This all started when Redick explained to Irving that he doesn't really think dinosaurs ever existed. He uses the examples that there isn't a full dinosaur body on display anywhere as an example of his skepticism, before asking Irving about his conspiracy theory beliefs, amongst other things.

Irving begins the interview by explaining his flat-earth views in more detail, before going into more detail about other strange and bizarre aspects of his life. He explains to J.J. Redick that he is a big believer in "spiritual alchemy," discussing in detail the different chakras you have as a human and the third eye that is in the middle of your forehead. All fascinating views, to say the least!

This takes the conversation onto Kyrie Irving's meditation practices, where he talks about enriching his soul and living in the physical realm, before making the claim that he feels more connected to Nikola Tesla through meditation.

He takes this crazy comment one step further by saying meditation has brought him closer to individuals in history that died before their time or might have even been murdered, the people in previous lives who have been deemed either geniuses or crazy people.

As a whole, this entire interview was full of crazy comments, but none more than saying that mediation has brought Irving closer to Nikola Tesla.

Chapter 5: Kyrie's Life Outside of Basketball

He Likes to Read

In October 2016, Kyrie Irving sat down with *Anything but Basketball*, to discuss his life outside of basketball. He was only 24 and playing for the Cleveland Cavaliers, but some interesting information about the man behind the player came out in this interview.

Kyrie Irving is a deep thinker, and he demonstrated this by stating that he enjoys reading and meditation when he isn't playing ball, and that he wants nothing more than to spend time with his family. He picked out some of the books that he reads in his spare time, and a lot is of them focused on better understanding your thoughts and feelings, and how to use that to your advantage to improve as a person.

His Biggest Personal Hurdle Away from Basketball was Fear

When discussing the journey of finding out about himself and what makes him tick as a person, Kyrie has always been quick to state that the journey began long before basketball, and he defines himself as much more than just a basketball player.

In an interview, Kyrie stated that one of his biggest personal hurdles that he is continually battling outside of basketball is the fear that if he isn't careful, he won't find the time to focus on himself and his own needs and he'll get swept up in what everyone else wants him to do or how everyone else wants him to act. His theory has always been that he can have a better impact on the world if he takes the time to become a better version of himself.

One thing that Kyrie has always tried to implement into his life as a basketballer, and outside of basketball, is to try and get used to being comfortable in uncomfortable situations. He has often spoken of a period in his early twenties where he admits he spent too much time worrying about what other people thought of him and being scared of failing. He also says he feared not being as educated as he should be in life, which is why he is so passionate about reading and researching outside of basketball.

He went on to explain in that interview that once he embraced fear and decided to stare it down and try to defeat it, all of a sudden, a world of possibilities inside and outside basketball opened up to him, and he overcame that hurdle and became more comfortable with who he is.

His Acting Career

During his time at the Boston Celtics, basketball wasn't the only thing on Kyrie Irving's radar, as his acting career began to blossom.

Kyrie Irving's interest in movies dates back to his time at high school. During his senior year, he was able to get himself a part in the school performance of "High School Musical."

Kyrie decided to audition for a part in the musical as he was scared of speaking in front of large crowds and decided the best way to overcome that fear was to jump in the deep end and audition for the yearly play that his school put on. Fortunately for Irving, he got a part, which allowed him to show people his singing voice and practice his acting skills in front of a live audience of his peers.

His acting career didn't end there though, as a few years later, early on in his NBA career, Kyrie Irving starred in a fun role as Uncle Drew, an elderly basketball player, as part of a short feature created by Pepsi Max. This short skit was so famous on social media that it developed several sequels, got cut and turned into on-air commercials, and even ended up becoming a feature film, where Irving reprised the role.

The film follows Uncle Drew, played by Irving, being drafted to play in a street ball tournament with a $100,000 cash prize for grabs. Uncle Drew recruits his team, selecting other Rucker Park legends and older players, before winning the tournament and the prize money.

The film went on to pick up several awards, including the Silver Award by Davey Awards and being nominated for best comedy at the Golden Trailer Awards.

In the same year, he is also attributed to being the voice of Vernon the Water Bear in an episode of Family Guy, further adding to his acting career.

Business Ventures

On top of his acting career, Irving also has a lucrative shoe deal with Nike, worth approximately $11 million as recently as 2019. His shoe deal with Nike is also one of the most successful ones in their history, becoming the second most successful sneaker line of 2017, second only to LeBron James.

As well as the usual sneaker collaborations, Kyrie Irving has also released a couple of themed collaborations as well, which included a *Friends* collaboration and a *Spongebob Squarepants* collaboration. So popular was the Spongebob Squarepants collaboration that it sold out within seconds of going live.

Kyrie Irving spoke to GQ when he launched the Spongebob Squarepants collaboration, explaining that he chose to debut them at a WNBA game rather than an NBA game to broaden the potential market for them, and to help shine a light on the women's game. He also revealed in that interview that the collaboration was his idea that he took to Nike, and so too was the idea to drop the release at a WNBA game. He talked about how much he loved *Spongebob Squarepants* as a child, and how he still watches it from time to time as an adult.

Family

As we already have discussed, Kyrie Irving enjoys reading in his spare time, as well as journaling his thoughts, singing, dancing, and even playing the baritone saxophone! He comes from NBA greatness, as his godfather is Rod Strickland, a former NBA player.

He has a daughter named Azure Elizabeth Irving with his ex-partner, who was born in November 2015. He gave her the middle name Elizabeth after his mother.

In May of 2011, Irving promised his father that he would go back to college and complete his bachelor's degree in the next five years, studying at Duke. Despite this promise, he had not achieved the feat by 2016, stating that at the time he was putting that task on hold, claiming that he would focus on that aspect of his life when basketball ended.

Irving is also known to get involved with several good causes. In November 2016, Kyrie Irving shared his support of the people at

Standing Rock Indian reservation who were protecting the water by tweeting out to his followers to raise awareness. The protectors were claiming that the pipe that the Dakota Access Pipeline built was violating treaty law, as it passed through sacred burial land at Standing Rock.

There was a severe level of concern as many thought the crude oil journeying through the pipeline could hamper the safety of the supply of drinking water that the Standing Rock community used, as did many other communities in the area, some Native and some non-native.

This was further backed up in August 2018, when Irving and his sister were offered a "welcome home" ceremony by the locals at Standing Rock to acknowledge the support they had shown their community. Irving's mother had been a member of the Standing Rock tribe and had lived there until she was adopted. Irving's grandmother and great-grandparents also had connections to the Standing Rock community.

Chapter 6: What's Next for Kyrie Irving?

So, where does Kyrie Irving go from here? What's next for one of the most talented current NBA players?

Brooklyn Nets

It is likely that Kyrie will want to start making his mark on his new team and putting in the performances that first got him into the national team. The last few seasons have seen him pick up several injuries that have either derailed successful seasons or prevented them from being as impressive as they might have been.

So first comes first, he will want to have a season where he remains fully fit throughout. Irving will also be keen to show he is maturing into the leader's role that he is so desperate to take on. His trade to the Nets from the Celtics was certainly controversial. However, there are clear signs that Irving is beginning to grow into the role of leader and is maturing as he gets older.

He has stated the importance of life outside of basketball, which shows he can balance the two, better than before. He has also spoken of his apology to LeBron for how he acted as a younger player, which likely means he now has a better grasp on what it takes to be a leader and how to manage players in his team that may act out as he did.

Ultimately, he will be looking to use these leadership skills and have a fully fit season to win another NBA championship. He is coming into his peak years as a player and based on his frustration when he is not in the limelight, Irving will want to show everyone why he should be discussed as one of the very best players.

If he can achieve all of this and keep his name out of the media for reasons other than winning games and being positive, then it is likely that he will quickly be talked about as one of the top players in the league once more.

The Fans Relationship

Another aspect of basketball that he will likely be keen to amend is his relationship with the fans. While he has never had issues with winning over fans of the franchise that he plays for, he has found it tougher to win over some of the general NBA fans.

His spat with LeBron James certainly didn't help matters, and neither did the acrimonious way that he left the Celtics for the Nets. However, the rest of the NBA fanbase is not lost. With a little bit of humility, and some smart press conferences added to some excellent basketball plays, he will quickly win the fans back onto his side as he did when he started his NBA career at the Cleveland Cavaliers.

USA Team

On the international stage, Kyrie Irving will be keen to try and make his way back into the national team if he can.

Given his age, he will likely be targeting one or two more FIBA world cups, and with the Olympics being postponed to 2021, he still has a chance to put a run of form and fitness together to break into that squad and try to add to his gold medal from the 2016 Olympics.

Acting

After Uncle Drew was a success in the box office, Kyrie Irving may be tempted to give acting another go in the near future. After all, basketball isn't forever, and he wouldn't be the first NBA star to transition into movies.

While he has stated he does not want to be seen as a celebrity, he has also indicated that he wants to run his own TV network in the past, so you would be foolish to rule anything out for Kyrie Irving!

Sneaker Line

After such a successful *Spongebob Squarepants* sneaker launch with Nike, don't be surprised to see some more Kyrie Irving kicks in the not-too-distant future. Still contracted to Nike, Irving will likely look to cash in again, although what the theme will be could be anyone's guess at this point.

Whatever he decides to release, they are sure to be a hit with the NBA and sneaker world!

Good Causes

After playing a role in helping look after the indigenous people of the Standing Rock Indian Reservation, it may be that Irving pursues other good causes for a similar impact. Given that he is an NBA star, his name carries weight, and his voice is often heard by many. That means whatever he puts his voice to will automatically garner more attention than it already has.

Conclusion

As you can see, there is a reason why Irving has quickly become one of the most talked-about players over the last decade! Despite his injuries and off-court incidents, he is still widely regarded as one of the very best point guards in the game, as he has proven himself time and time again on the court!

Over the years, he has become more outspoken in the media, although he will be hoping to have put that controversial side of his career behind him, after signing a long-term contract with the Nets. This long-term contract should stop reporters from constantly hounding him about his future, which should allow Irving to focus more on his basketball than on the celebrity lifestyle element that comes with being an NBA player these days.

On the court, Irving will be hoping to get fit and lead the Nets to an NBA championship.

There are many opportunities for Kyrie Irving lying ahead, which is particularly exciting given his incredible talent on the court!

I hope you have enjoyed learning about Kyrie Irving, and have a new appreciation for the basketball superstar and all that he has achieved thus far!

www.ingramcontent.com/pod-product-compliance
Lightning Source LLC
LaVergne TN
LVHW021736060526
838200LV00052B/3308